Margery

Melody

Marty

Micky

MEERKAT MISCHIEF

Milly

Monty

Grandpa

Mariella

The Triplets

Molly and Mimi

Magenta

Buster Books

Written by Lottie Stride

Illustrated by Alex Paterson

Edited by Elizabeth Scoggins and Hannah Cohen

Designed by Barbara Ward and Angie Allison

First published in Great Britain in 2011 by Buster Books,
an imprint of Michael O'Mara Books Limited,
9 Lion Yard, Tremadoc Road, London SW4 7NQ

A CIP catalogue record for this book is available from the British Library.

ISBN: 978-1-78055-009-1

2 4 6 8 10 9 7 5 3 1

www.mombooks.com/busterbooks

This book was printed in August 2011 at Shenzhen Wing King Tong Paper Products Co., Ltd., Shenzhen, Guangdong, China

Papers used by Michael O'Mara Books are natural, recyclable products made from wood grown in sustainable forests. The manufacturing processes conform to the environmental regulations of the country of origin.

CONTENTS

MEET MONTY!

HELLO, I'M MONTY.
Welcome to the amazing world of meerkats. Meerkats are small, furry mammals that live in the deserts of Africa. We often have large families. Turn the pages to meet mine!

SNACK SPOTTER!
Monty loves to nibble grubs like these. There are 16 more of them hiding in this book. See if you can spot them all. The answers are on page **64**.

Yum yum!

The grubs all look like this.

MONTY'S SUDOKU CHALLENGE

Monty has a puzzle for you. There are four tasty meerkat treats in the puzzle opposite, but can you complete the grid, so that each row, each column and each block of four squares contains one each of the treats below? The answer is on page **62**.

A lizard.   A snake.   A banana.   An egg.

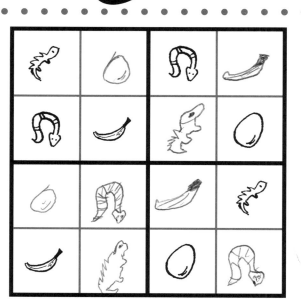

MEERKAT QUIZ

How much do you already know about meerkats? Why not try this quiz and find out?

Circle one answer for each question, then check your answers on page 62.

1. How long do meerkats usually live?
   a. 12-14 seconds   **b.** 12-14 days   **c.** 12-14 years

2. Which of these is about the same height as a meerkat?
   a. A pencil sharpener   **b.** A 30-centimetre ruler
   c. The Eiffel Tower, Paris

3. Which of these creatures is a meerkat most in danger of being attacked by?
   a. A hawk   **b.** An alien   **c.** A hamster

4. Which of these is the place you are most likely to find meerkats?
   a. Central Park, New York   **b.** Kalahari Desert, Southern Africa
   c. Under your bed

5. Which of these only takes a meerkat a few seconds to do?
   a. Turn a cartwheel   **b.** Move its own weight in sand
   c. Eat an elephant

6. A meerkat is a type of which animal?
   a. A mongoose   **b.** A hippo   **c.** A llama

DID YOU KNOW?
Meerkats have lots of black fur around their eyes to help cut out the glare from the strong desert sun.

PICTURE THIS

Have a go at drawing your own picture of Monty in the big grid on this page.

Use a pencil to copy what you see in each square in the small grid below into the same square on the big grid on the right. Then go over the lines in pen and use felt-tip pens to finish your picture.

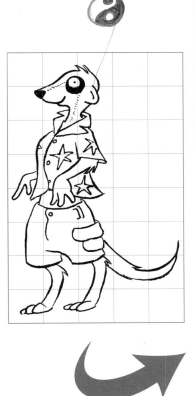

JUGGLING WITH GRANDPA

Meet Monty's Grandpa – the world-famous juggling meerkat! Grandpa has some useful tips on juggling, so follow his instructions on these pages to find out more.

1. Start with just one ball. Stand with your arms bent and your hands shoulder-width apart.

2. Throw the ball from one hand to the other, and back. On every throw, try to make the ball follow an arc-shape roughly 20 cm (8 in) from your chest, just above your eye-height.

3. Keep going until you can throw and catch the ball in the same way every time without thinking.

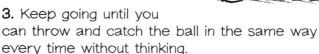

This is called the 'exchange'.

4. Now add an extra ball. Hold one in each hand, and throw the first ball up just like you did in step **2**.

5. When it's just above eye-height and is about to come down, throw the second ball.

This leaves your hand empty just in time to catch the first ball.

Keep trying over and over again until you get into a rhythm.

6. Now you can try three balls. Hold two balls in one hand and one in the other. Throw the first ball, then throw the second ball just before you catch the first, just like you did in step **5**. This time you need to throw the third ball just before you catch the second.

Step **6** will take a bit of time to get right. It helps if you keep your eyes straight ahead, looking at the top of your throws. And remember – try and try again. You'll get there!

Once you've managed three passes in a row, you are juggling!

This is called a 'pass'.

SPOT THE TIE

Grandpa likes to entertain the meerkat triplets with his juggling, but can you find the matching bow tie for his outfit? The answer is on page 62.

A   B   C

D   E   F

DOT-TO-DOT

Join all the dots in the right order and find out
who's drinking at the water hole with the meerkats.
The answer is on page 62.

MEERKAT ROULETTE

This dice game is popular with Monty and his family on freezing desert evenings.

HOW TO PLAY

The aim of the game is for each player to draw each section of a meerkat in sequence. You must roll the dice, in order, from one to six to finish your drawing.

1. Before the game begins, all players take a turn at throwing the dice. The player with the highest score is the one who starts the first round of the game.

2. In the first round, every player takes it in turn to throw the dice once, starting with the person who threw the highest score.

In this round, any player who throws a 'one' can start his or her drawing.

Any player who doesn't throw a 'one', has to try again in the next round.

When you throw a 'three', you can draw the ears.

When you throw a 'four', you can draw the arms.

DRAWING ORDER

When you throw a 'one', you can draw the meerkat's body and legs, as shown.

When you throw a 'five', you can draw the face.

When you throw a 'six', you can draw the tail.

When you throw a 'two', you can draw the head.

3. The winner is the first player to complete their drawing of the meerkat in the correct order.

MOVIE MAYHEM

A film crew has come to the desert in search of animals to film – the meerkats are going to be in the movies! All the answers to these puzzles are on page 62.

BAFFLING BALLS

Grandpa Meerkat thinks his juggling skills are worthy of the big screen and is showing off in front of the camera. But can you find the three matching pairs of balls, and spot the one that is unique?

A 'PROP-ER' MIX-UP

The meerkats have muddled up the movie props in the prop cupboard. Can you put them back where they should be and complete the grid so that each row, each column and each block of four squares contains one each of the props below?

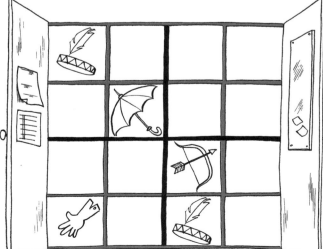

A feather headdress.

A parasol.

A bow and arrow.

A glove.

12

The twins, Mimi and Molly Meerkat, have sneaked into the crew's canteen and helped themselves to an ice-cream sundae each. Can you work out which they had?

WIRE SCRAMBLE

The meerkats have been running around the set and have tangled up the wires. Can you untangle the wires to work out which piece of film-making equipment is connected to which electrical socket?

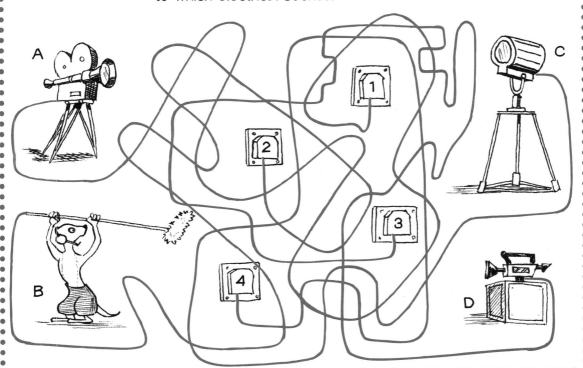

GINGERBREAD MEERKATS

These gingerbread meerkats make a truly scrumptious snack. Read on to find out how to make them.

YOU WILL NEED:

- tracing paper
- 75 g (5 tablespoons) softened butter
- 50 g (3 ½ tablespoons) caster sugar (superfine sugar)
- 2 egg yolks
- 1 teaspoon baking powder
- 50 g (3 ½ tablespoons) golden syrup
- 250 g (1 cup) plain, sifted flour
- 2 tablespoons ground ginger
- 1 teaspoon ground cinnamon
- plastic wrap
- a tube of writing icing.

Meerkat Template

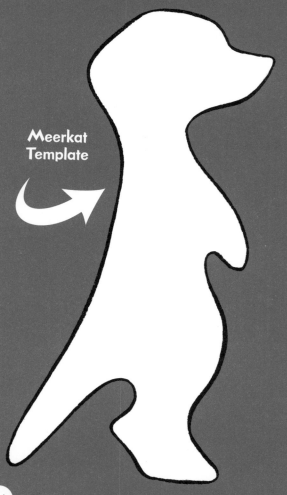

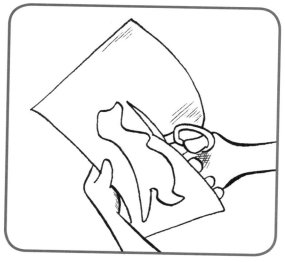

1. Place your tracing paper over the meerkat template on the left and trace around the outline.

Cut it out and put it to one side.

14

2. Cream the butter and sugar together in a bowl, add the egg yolks, baking powder and syrup and mix well.

3. Stir in the flour, ginger and cinnamon and mix well until it forms a dough.

4. Place the dough in plastic wrap and chill it for half an hour.

5. Ask an adult to preheat the oven to 180 °C/350 °F/Gas mark 4.

6. Sprinkle some flour on to a clean surface, then roll out the dough until it's about ½ cm (¼ in) thick.

7. Place the traced outline of the meerkat on top of the dough and carefully cut around it with a knife.

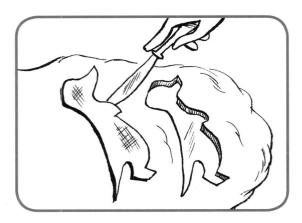

8. Repeat until you have lots of meerkats and no dough left.

9. Use a spatula to carefully place each meerkat shape on to a greased baking tray, then ask an adult to help you put it in the oven for 10 minutes, or until they are golden brown.

10. Ask an adult to help you remove the tray from the oven and place the meerkats on a wire rack to cool.

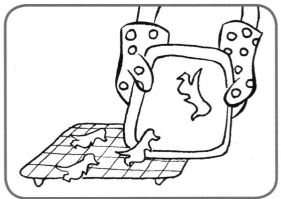

11. Once the meerkats are completely cool, use the tube of writing icing to give each cute meerkat features.

MELODY MEERKAT
AND HER ORCHESTRA!

CAN YOU SPOT THE DIFFERENCE?

Melody Meerkat started up the first meerkat orchestra
in Southern Africa. But can you spot 15 differences between
these two pictures? The answers are on page **62**.

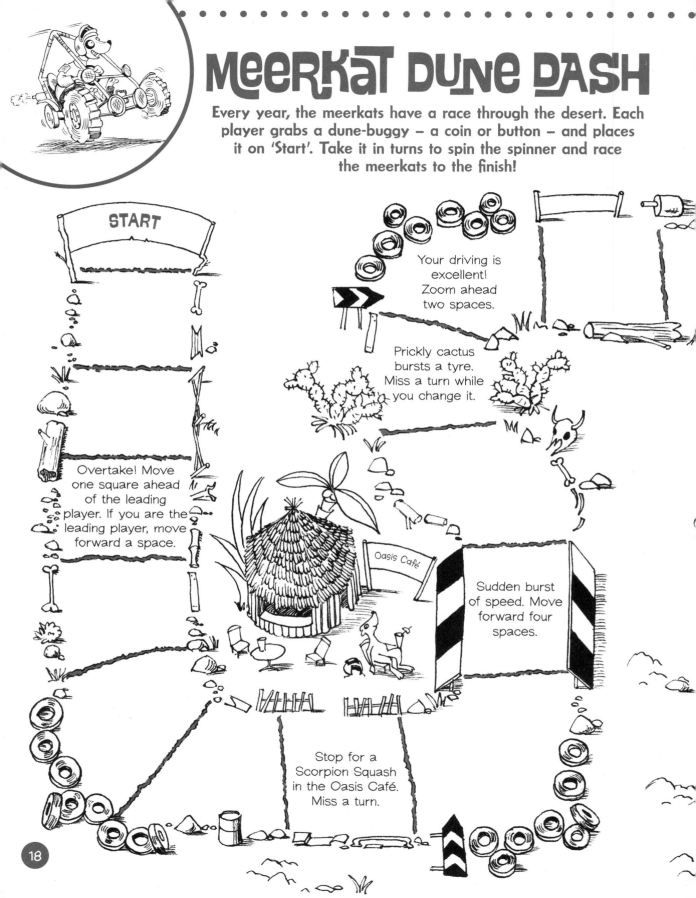

MEERKAT DUNE DASH

Every year, the meerkats have a race through the desert. Each player grabs a dune-buggy – a coin or button – and places it on 'Start'. Take it in turns to spin the spinner and race the meerkats to the finish!

START

Your driving is excellent! Zoom ahead two spaces.

Prickly cactus bursts a tyre. Miss a turn while you change it.

Overtake! Move one square ahead of the leading player. If you are the leading player, move forward a space.

Oasis Café

Sudden burst of speed. Move forward four spaces.

Stop for a Scorpion Squash in the Oasis Café. Miss a turn.

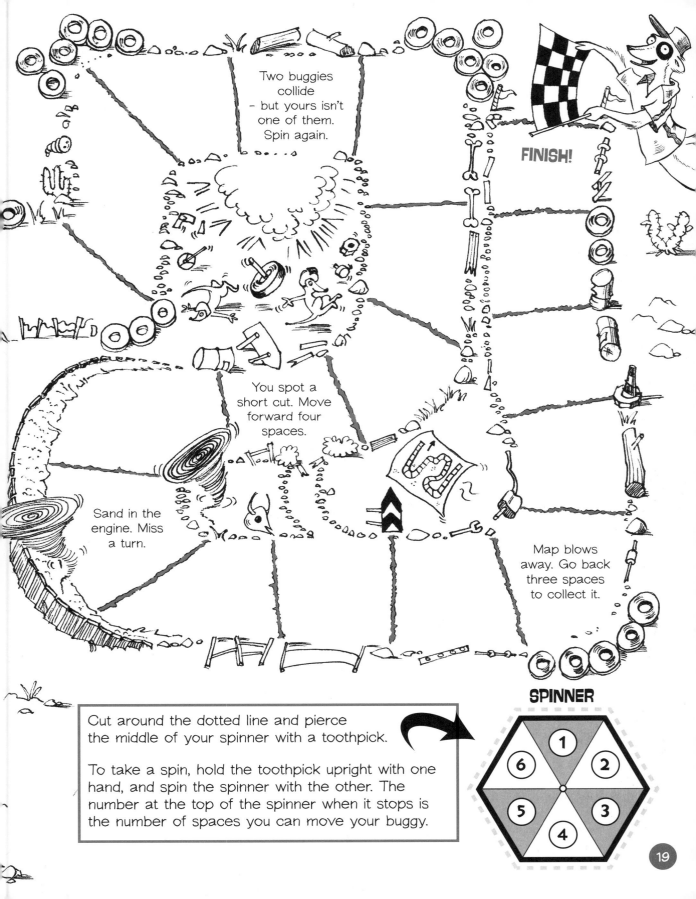

Two buggies collide - but yours isn't one of them. Spin again.

FINISH!

You spot a short cut. Move forward four spaces.

Sand in the engine. Miss a turn.

Map blows away. Go back three spaces to collect it.

SPINNER

Cut around the dotted line and pierce the middle of your spinner with a toothpick.

To take a spin, hold the toothpick upright with one hand, and spin the spinner with the other. The number at the top of the spinner when it stops is the number of spaces you can move your buggy.

1 2 3 4 5 6

Decorate the hot-air balloon and fill the sky with birds.

DESERT MUDDLE

Can you help Monty get to the meerkat triplets? He can only pass through fountains of fire but must avoid any of the spiralling sandswirls. Then help them all make their way back to the burrow, passing only through the spiralling sandswirls but avoiding fountains of fire. The answer is on page **62**.

THE BURROW

21

SPOT THE MEERKATS

Fifteen meerkats have sneaked into this theme park.
Can you spot them all? The answer is on page 63.

HaWKS OR MEERKatS?

Why not play this exciting game of meerkat chase with your friends? You need two 'bases' to play it. The easiest bases to use are playground walls, but you can mark out a base using coats, or use the space between two trees or pieces of equipment. Here's how to play:

1. Choose one person to be a Hawk. Everyone else is a Meerkat.

2. The Hawk stands at the mid-point between the two bases. The Meerkats line up along the first base.

3. The Hawk shouts 'GO!', and the Meerkats run to the other base.

4. If the Hawk touches a Meerkat, the Meerkat squeaks and goes to the middle. Now the Meerkat turns into a Hawk too, and starts trying to touch the running Meerkats.

5. If a Meerkat reaches the other base without being touched, he or she counts to ten, then starts running back to the first base.

6. The game carries on until every Meerkat but one has been caught and turned into a Hawk.

7. The last Meerkat caught is the winner.

THE RULES

- Once you start running, keep going – no turning back.
- Once you finish counting to ten, go – no waiting.
- If you do turn back, or wait too long, you must join the Hawks.

TIPS FOR MEERKATS
Wait until the Hawk is distracted by chasing another meerkat. Every meerkat for itself!

TIPS FOR HAWKS
See if you can intercept a Meerkat on the way to the opposite base.

THE UPSIDE-DOWN TREE

'Time for a walk, Monty,' said Grandpa.

'Yippee!' said the young meerkat.

Monty loved walks with his Grandpa. Grandpa always told him amazing stories about the things they saw.

Today, Grandpa stopped in front of a big tree. 'This is a baobab tree, Monty,' he said.

Monty looked up. 'Grandpa,' he said, 'that's the strangest tree I've ever seen.' The baobab towered above him, its big, wide trunk stretching high into the sky and, at the top, lots of spreading root-like branches.

'We meerkats call it the upside-down tree,' smiled Grandpa. 'And let me tell you why.'

Monty shivered with delight. Grandpa was going to tell another one of his stories!

'Long, long ago,' Grandpa began, 'back when the Earth was young, the baobab tree was the first tree to appear. Then came the flame tree, glowing with dazzling flowers, and the fig tree, bursting with glorious fruits.

'The baobab felt unhappy. It went to the Gods and complained. "Why don't I have such bright flowers?" it said. "Why aren't my branches loaded with plump, juicy fruits?"

'Day after day after day, the baobab tree grumbled. Every morning, from sunrise to sunset, the noise of the baobab tree complaining filled the air.

'"Enough!" said the Gods. "We will listen no longer." Then the Gods pulled the baobab tree right out of the ground – and replanted it upside down. At last, the baobab tree was silent.'

DRAWING MeeRKaTS

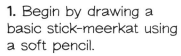

Learn how to draw your own meerkat and make your own meerkat mischief!

1. Begin by drawing a basic stick-meerkat using a soft pencil.

Draw a circle for the head and two ovals – one for the chest and one for the meerkat's bottom.

Add a line for the neck, a line for the back and two zigzagging lines for the meerkat's legs.

2. Fill out your meerkat by adding a pointy nose and curved lines for the sides of the neck and body, as shown here.

3. When you're happy with the shape of your meerkat's body and head, rub out the lines on the inside.

4. Fatten up one of your meerkat's legs, as shown here. The leg should be much wider at the top than it is at the bottom.

5. Erase the lines on the inside of your meerkat's leg, then fatten up the other leg, as shown.

6. Add one arm coming from the right shoulder, bent at the elbow. Then add the other arm, peeping out from the other side of your meerkat's body, as shown here.

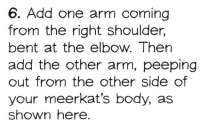

7. Draw a large, black spot for your meerkat's nose, and add a round eye with a black circle around it.

8. Draw a half oval on the end of each arm for hands, adding fingers, as shown here in close-up.

9. Erase the lines inside your meerkat's hands, add toes and draw in a long tail.

10. Lastly, to give your meerkat some character, add a smiley mouth, rounded ears and tufts of fur.

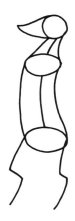
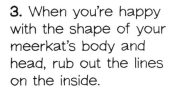

Once you've got the hang of it, turn the page and discover how to add your meerkat to your own comic-strip caper.

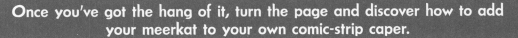

MEERKAT TO THE RESCUE!

Once you've mastered drawing your own meerkat (see page 25) you'll be super-ready to draw Marty, trainee superhero meerkat! Follow the instructions below, and draw your own Marty the Meerkat in the big box on the opposite page.

(see page 25)

YOU WILL NEED:

- tracing paper
- rough paper
- a pencil
- a black pen
- an eraser
- felt-tip pens.

1. Use a pencil to build up the basic shapes of Marty's head, body and legs. Try to copy the shapes in the first picture shown on the right, as closely as you can.

2. Erase the unnecessary lines on the inside of the body.

3. Next add a C-shape for the ear, a large black dot for the nose, and a round eye with a black circle around it.

4. Finish off the face with a curl of hair and a big, smiling mouth.

5. Fill out the shape of the arms and add a tail.

Copy the shape of the hands as closely as you can to get Marty's pose just right.

6. Add tufts and shading to Marty's fur.

7. Draw in the shape of a superhero cape going over Marty's shoulders.

Add lines for his costume and add a superhero emblem on his chest.

Why not make Marty the star of his very own comic strip?

I can fly!

Wey-hey!

Oof!

What happens next?

MONTY'S DREAM

Monty is dreaming about an amazing adventure in space, but can you put all the dream bubbles in the right order? Turn to page 63 to check your answer. The first one has been done for you.

The correct sequence is:

1. G
2. ....
3. ....
4. ....
5. ....
6. ....
7. ....

What else have the mischievous meerkats brought home to their burrow? Doodle your ideas.

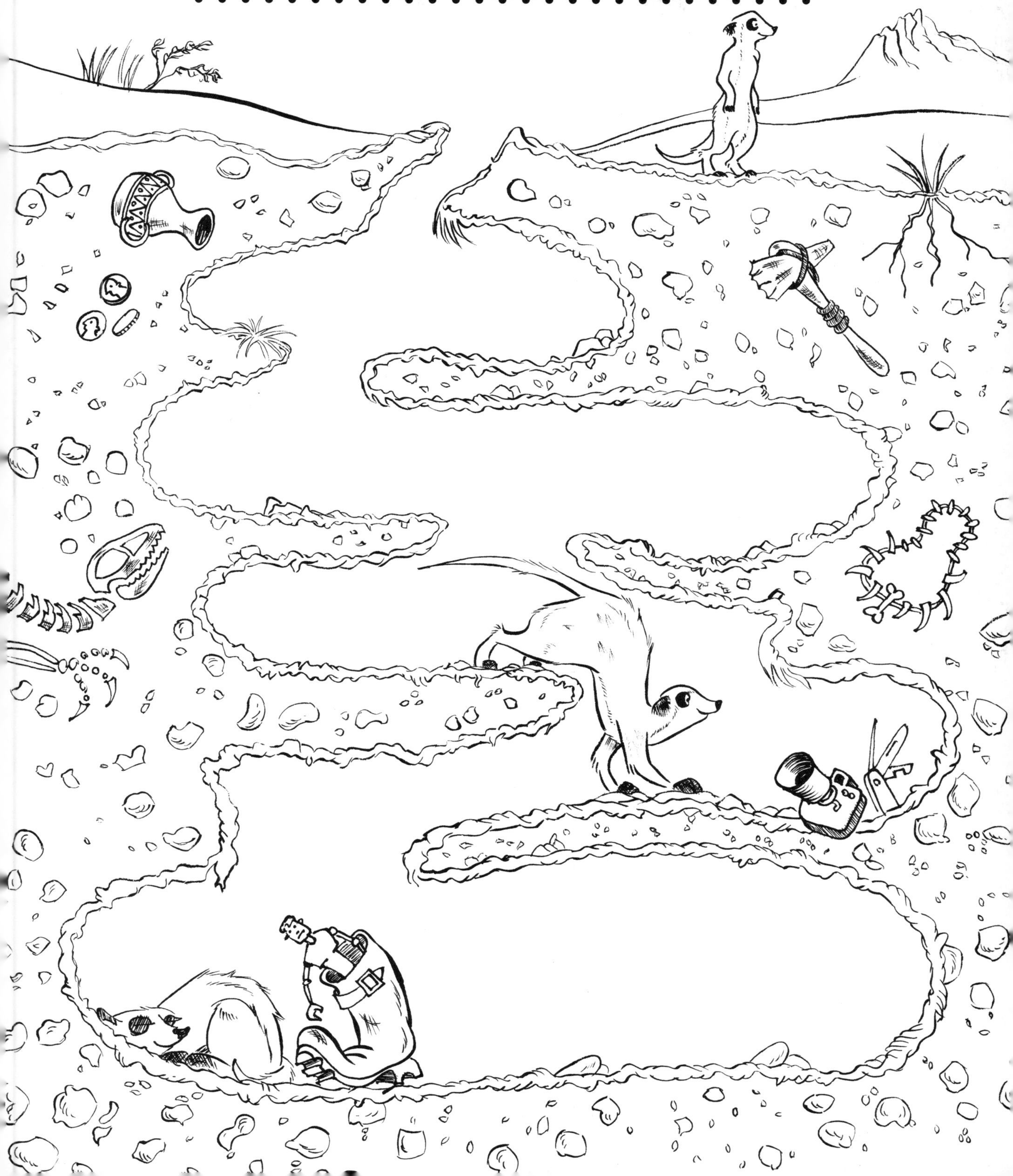

PARTY TIME!

It's Grandpa's birthday today, and he's having a big family party. Once you've worked the puzzles out, check your answers on page 63.

DANCING DOUBLES

Only two of these dancing meerkats are identical twins, Mimi and Molly. Can you spot which ones?

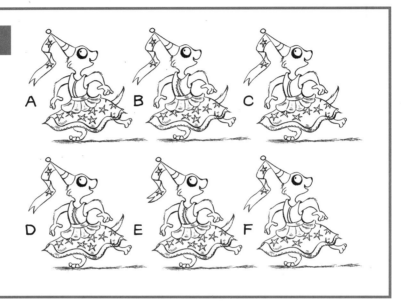

A   B   C

D   E   F

TREAT TRACKING

The meerkats are running out of party food, so Monty has been sent out to hunt down some extra tasty treats. Can you help him find the things on his list?

3 lizards
5 snakes
12 fruits

SURPRISE!

Join the dots to find out what animal is bursting out of Grandpa's giant cake to join in the meerkat family fun.

MEERKAT MOBILES

One of the meerkat triplets has made a kite mobile and a star mobile to hang in the meerkat burrow. Why not have a go at making some yourself?

KITE MOBILE

1. Trace the outline of the kite-shape, shown on the opposite page, then cut it out to make a template.

2. Place your template in the corner of your sheet of card and draw around it. Do this four more times, then cut out each shape.

3. Decorate both sides of each kite-shape any way you like, then cut five strips of ribbon about 15 cm (6 ins) long.

Glue one to the bottom of each kite, to make the tails, as shown here.

YOU WILL NEED:

- tracing paper
- a sheet of thin A4 (8 by 11 ins) card
- scissors
- a narrow piece of ribbon, measuring 1 m (3 ft) long
- a ball of wool or string
- a wire coathanger
- a tube of all-purpose glue
- a selection of paints, crayons or pencils.

TOP TIP

For an extra-special kite tail, make bow-shapes out of card and stick them along the ribbon, like this.

4. Glue string to the top of each kite, making each piece a different length. Tie your kites to the hanger, and space them out.

5. Work out where you want to hang your mobile. Tie string to the hook of the hanger and ask an adult to help you hang it up.

Once it's hanging, you may need to move the kites around a bit until the mobile balances.

YOU WILL NEED:

- drinking straws (not the bendy kind)
- paperclips
- sticky tape
- tracing paper
- a sheet of thin A4 (8 by 11 ins) card
- scissors
- a selection of paints, crayons or pencils.

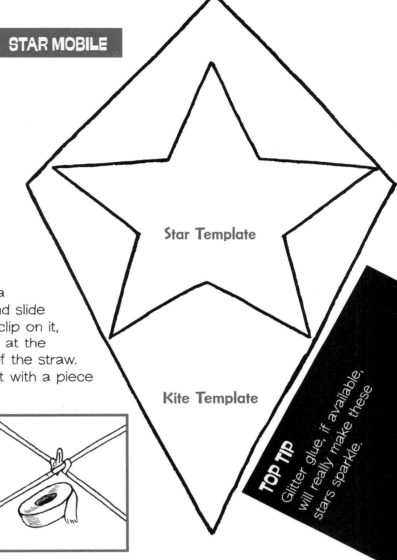

Star Template

Kite Template

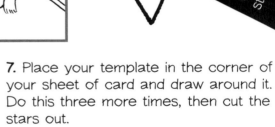

TOP TIP
Glitter glue, if available, will really make these stars sparkle.

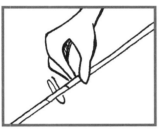

1. Take a straw and slide a paperclip on it, stopping at the middle of the straw. Secure it with a piece of tape.

2. Now take another straw and place it directly beneath the paperclip, crossing the other straw. Secure with a long piece of tape, as shown here.

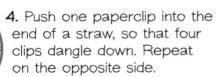

3. Next make two paperclip chains that are each five paperclips long.

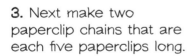

4. Push one paperclip into the end of a straw, so that four clips dangle down. Repeat on the opposite side.

5. Make two more paperclip chains, this time measuring seven clips long, and push them into opposite ends of the other straw.

6. Next trace the outline of the star-shape, shown opposite, then cut it out to make a template.

7. Place your template in the corner of your sheet of card and draw around it. Do this three more times, then cut the stars out.

8. Decorate both sides of each star.

9. Once all your paints are dry, slide a star on to the end of each paperclip chain, so that they hang down.

10. To hang the mobile, make another chain and attach it to the paperclip in the middle of your mobile. Get an adult to help you hang it up.

Doodle more meerkat babies playing in the sand.

RECORD HOLDERS

Meerkats love to compare each other's achievements and hold competitions to discover who's the best! Help them continue their comparisons, checking your answers on page 63.

MEDAL MIX-UP

Monty's prizewinning aunties and uncles have got their medals muddled. Can you match the medal to the meerkat?

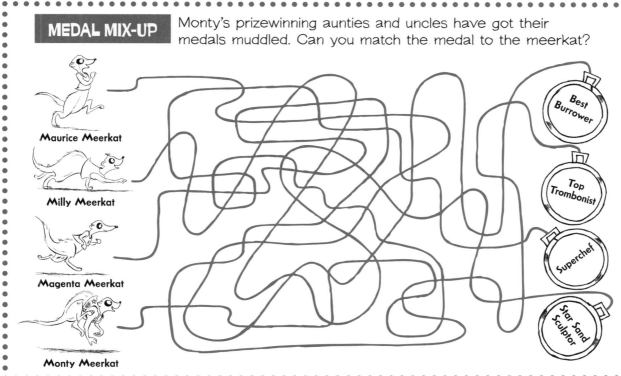

Maurice Meerkat

Milly Meerkat

Magenta Meerkat

Monty Meerkat

Best Burrower

Top Trombonist

Superchef

Star Sand Sculptor

WHO'S TALLEST?

The meerkats can't decide who's tallest – but can you? Use the clues below to work it out, then tick one box in the table for each of them. Each meerkat is a different height.

Magenta is only taller than Maurice.

Milly is shorter than Monty.

Monty is taller than Magenta.

Milly is taller than Maurice.

	25 cm (10 in)	28 cm (11 in)	30 cm (12 in)	33 cm (13 in)
Magenta				
Maurice				
Milly				
Monty				

HOW THE MEERKAT MARVELS BEGAN

Every day, the meerkats took it in turns to be lookouts. While other meerkats played and foraged and groomed each other, the lookouts checked for hawks and eagles swooping through the sky in search of a meerkat dinner. Today, it was Molly and Micky's turn.

'It's not fair,' said Molly Meerkat. 'Being lookout is boring. And hot. And dusty.'

Micky, her brother, heaved a big sigh. 'You know what?' he said. 'We've been standing here for hours and what have we seen? Nothing.'

Molly had an idea. 'I know, let's pretend there really is a hawk coming to eat us up,' she said.

'Good idea!' said Micky. Then Molly and Micky both started yelling at the top of their voices. 'Hawk! Hawk! Hawk!' From every direction, meerkats heard the warning and scampered for the safety of the burrow.

When Grandpa realized what mischief Molly and Micky were up to he told them sternly, 'Do NOT do that again'.

But Molly and Micky did. Three more times that day they yelled, 'Hawk! Hawk! Hawk!' Three more times the meerkats heard the warning and scampered for the safety of the burrow.

Grandpa was cross. He made Micky tidy up the camp. He sent Molly off to the higher ground to look for some roots to add to a stew. But as Molly searched she saw a shadow swoop through the sky ... a dark shadow ... heading for the meerkat burrow!

Molly charged back towards the burrow. 'Hawk!' she yelled, at the top of her voice. 'Hawk!' But no one believed her. No one took cover – and the hawk swooped into the camp.

'Oh no! Micky!' Molly gasped, as she skidded through the scrub and into camp. She watched, horrified, as the hawk swooped down and grabbed Micky in its great claws, then took off.

'Help!' yelled Micky, dangling down, terrified. Molly took the biggest leap of her life. She grabbed hold of Micky's flailing paws and clung on.

The three of them swooped through the air. The hawk holding Micky in its claws, Molly clinging on to Micky's paws, the ground far, far below.

Then Molly saw a patch of trees coming up ahead. 'I've got an idea!' yelled Molly. 'Copy me!' She started swinging her body backwards and forwards, swinging further and further each time. Micky did the same. The hawk didn't like it. It started screeching. Its wings started wobbling ... and then ... it let go of Micky.

Down, down, down, Molly and Micky went. The trees came rushing towards them. 'Swing through the branches and down to the ground,' yelled Molly. 'Don't think about it, just do it!'

So Molly and Micky went swinging down through the trees, grabbing first one branch, then another, going lower and lower until, at last, they landed.

Back home they told the story of their amazing acrobatic escape. Grandpa smiled. 'That gives me an idea,' he said. 'A way to keep you two out of mischief!'

A week later, Molly and Micky started their first day at Circus Skills School. And so, the Meerkat Marvels began.

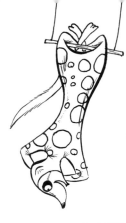

JiGSaW JUMBLE

This jigsaw is of the Meerkat Marvels doing their astonishing aerial acrobatics. But some pieces from another jigsaw have got mixed in with it. Can you work out which three pieces fit the gaps? The answer is on page 63.

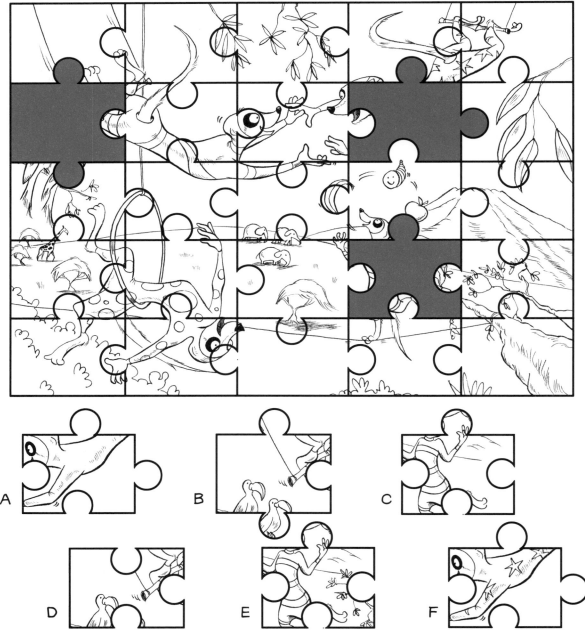

MEERKAT-ROBATICS!

The Meerkat Marvels have been performing their incredible jumps and tumbles
in front of amazed audiences since they were tiny pups.
And you can, too with a little practice.

GETTING STARTED

1. Place a ring of string or a hoop on the ground. Jump in and out of it 20 times.

2. Place two sheets of newspaper on a carpeted floor or grass and use them as stepping stones to move between two points. Each time you take a step, pick up the piece of paper behind you and move it forwards to take the next step.

3. Next, walk on your hands for two 'steps'. (This may take a few tries to perfect!)

4. Follow this with three cartwheels in a row.

5. Tape a piece of string or ribbon across a doorway, or between two trees, then do a crabwalk underneath it to finish.

Use these ideas to make your own acrobatics course on a soft floor in your house or on some grass in the garden or at the park.

MEERKATS ON HOLIDAY

Monty and the meerkats are on holiday. But can you solve these summer-time puzzlers? All the answers are on page 63.

All the answers are on page 63.

HOW TO PLAY

Each of these four circles represents a holiday sport. The letters represent all Monty's family on the holiday.

Where the circles cross each other, the meerkat inside likes more than one kind of holiday sport. For example, meerkat D likes waterskiing and volleyball, but he doesn't like hang gliding or snorkelling.

1. Can you work out who likes hang gliding, waterskiing and snorkelling, but not volleyball?

2. Who would play volleyball or go snorkelling but not waterskiing or hang gliding?

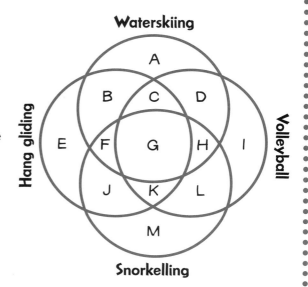

MATCH IT!

Help Monty and the meerkat triplets find the beach towels that match their costumes.

40

WHODUNNIT?

Oops! Someone threw the beach ball and smashed Grandpa's plate of Grub 'n' Chips. Can you follow the trail to work out who threw it?

MILLY'S MEERMAID

Milly has entered the meermaid sand sculpture competition. But can you spot which one is hers? Here are some clues:

- Milly's meermaid sculpture has long hair.
- The meermaid's hair is not curly.
- The meermaid doesn't have a shell in her hair.
- The meermaid's necklace does have a pendant on it.

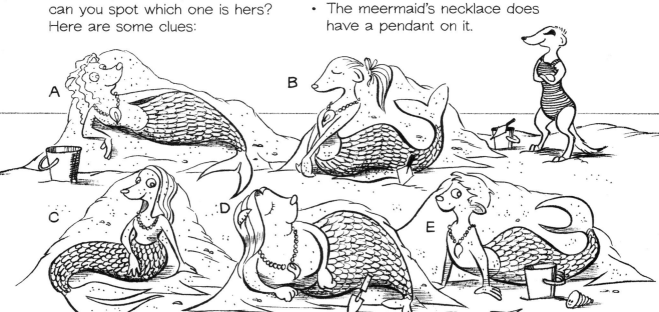

Use paints, crayons or felt-tip pens to decorate this surfing scene.

CRAFTY CRITTER

For hours of meerkat mischief, find out how to make a crafty critter that sits perfectly on your desk or shelf.

1. Use pencils and pens to decorate the body and the head shapes on this page however you like. You might cover them in brown fur or you might want to give them a bright makeover.

Turn the page to find out how to cut out your crafty critter and make it come to life.

Meerkat Head Shape

Meerkat Body Shape

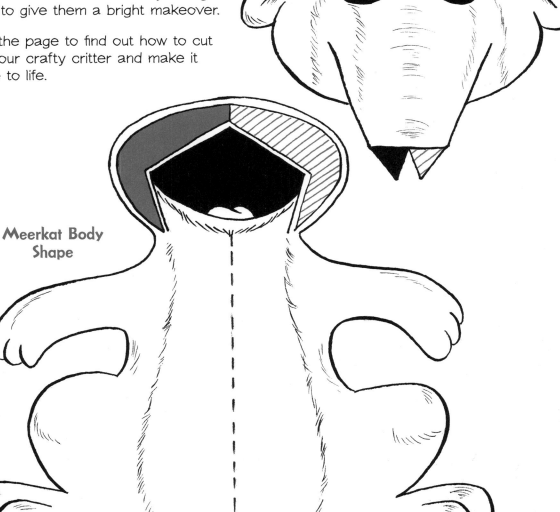

2. Finish decorating the body and head shapes below then cut out both shapes along the solid outside lines.

3. Fold the body down the middle, so that its tail is on the outside, then open the body out again, until it stands up by itself.

4. Pinch the black diagonal lines on the head, then bend up the nose, overlap the triangles at the end and glue them together.

Add glue here.

5. Fold the head in half with the design on the inside. Put glue on the striped area on the inside of the body shape, and press the striped area of the head on to it.

6. Glue the other side of the head to the body, where marked, and leave to dry.

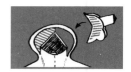

7. Finally, stand up your crafty critter, like so:

Cut along the solid lines here.

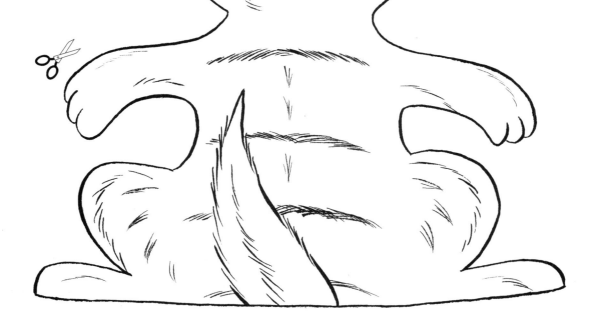

GRANDPA'S ISLAND PUZZLER

Grandpa, Maurice and Milly have gone on an island adventure!
After a day playing in the sand however, Grandpa has a tricky problem on
his hands. Can you work out a way that he can solve the problem below?
The answer is on page 64.

GRANDPA'S TRICKY LOGIC CHALLENGE

Grandpa went to the island with Maurice and Milly Meerkat. He's found a giant coconut, and he needs to get himself, Maurice and Milly back to the mainland with the coconut. But the boat is only large enough to carry him and one other thing, so he'll have to make more than one trip.

Grandpa's got two problems though. First, he can't leave Maurice alone with Milly, as he'll pull her ears and makes her cry. Second, he can't leave Milly alone with the coconut, as she'll eat it all. Maurice – although he teases – isn't greedy, so he can be left alone with the coconut.

DOT-TO-DOT CHALLENGE

While Grandpa Meerkat is working out what to do, Maurice and Milly are teasing each other, but what is hidden in this picture? The answer is on page **64**.

WILDERNESS EXPLORERS!

MEET MARGERY MEERKAT, FAMOUS EXPLORER

Margery meets all sorts of creatures on her travels around the world. She has set some tricky puzzlers for Monty – can you help him work out the answers? Turn to page 64 to check if you're right.

STARRY, STARRY NIGHT

At night, the desert sky is full of stars. But can you spot the 22 stars in this picture?

Clue: not all the stars are in the sky!

SILHOUETTE SCRAMBLE

Margery has been helping Monty learn how to track - can you unscramble the names of these desert animals and match them to the correct silhouette to work out what they have been following?

1. CIOPSRNO

2. ZRLIDA

3. SMUOE

4. KANSE

. . . .

A

B

C

D

BIRD BONANZA

Margery has been spotting birds - she's drawn up a map of the area showing all the birds she's found there. Can you spot these six birds and write down their co-ordinates?

To find the co-ordinates, write down the letter of the row and the number of the column in which it appears.

For example, there is a Tuft-headed hen in **B6**.

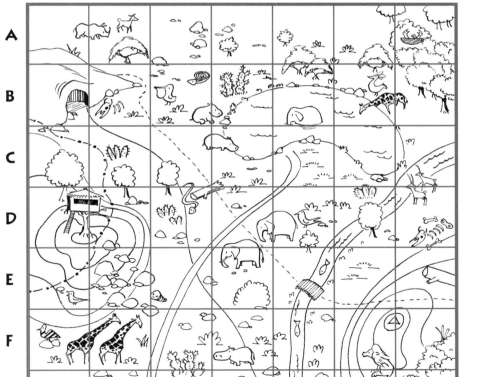

1. Two-tailed swift

2. Striped starling

3. Talking tit

4. Pouched hummingbird

5. Baby sparrows

6. Long-legged vulture

HiDE AND SEEK

Monty is playing hide and seek with the meerkat triplets. He has Margery's compass and some clues to where to find them. Can you follow Monty's route on the map below and help him work out where they are?
The answer is on page 64.

Do you think the triplets are hiding behind cactus A, B, C, D or E?

- Head north until you reach the furthest cactus from Monty's starting point.
- Then head east until you have passed the waterhole.
- Now go south until you reach a cactus on its own.

START HERE

Draw what is making
the meerkat triplets laugh.

SPYKAT!

The meerkats are bored at school, so their teacher has asked Mariella Meerkat, famous spy, to visit. She's got some top tips for some brain-stretching puzzles.
All the answers are on page 64.

BRAIN TRAINING

Mariella has set some brain-training coded calculations to get everyone started. Each spy symbol stands for a number. Can you figure out the answers and draw in the missing symbols?

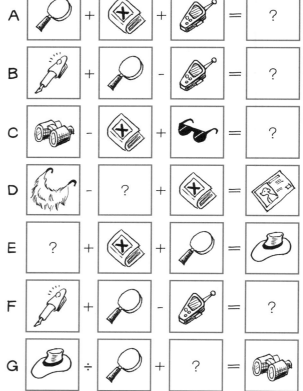

CODE CRACKING

Mariella has coded some messages. But be warned – she's made them tricky to decode. She's jumbled up the spaces and she's also using two different codes. In some messages, she replaces each letter with a letter two places forward in the alphabet. So A becomes C and so on. In others, she replaces each letter in the message with a letter three places forward in the alphabet.

Why not test out your decoding skills against some friends? First to decode them all is top spy!

1. OCRKU WPFG THN QYGT RQV

2. WU XVW QRRQH

3. QDPHRI WUDL WRULV VPLWK

4. CV VCEM FCVGKU VWG UFCA

NUMB3R CODES

Spies use number codes as well as
letter codes. To start, replace each
letter of the alphabet with a number.
So A becomes 1, B becomes 2, all the
way through to Z, which is 26.

Use this code to work out what
this means:

20, 8, 5   6, 1, 12, 3, 15, 14   8, 1, 19
6, 12, 15, 23, 14   20, 8, 5   14, 5, 19, 20.

To make your code more complicated
- and more secretive - start
numbering from the first letter of your
name. For example, if your name is
Marvin, M is 1, N is 2, all the way to
Z, which is 14. A then becomes 15,
B becomes 16, and so on.

**Write your answer in
Mariella's magnifying glass.**

MARIELLA'S CODE-BREAKING TIPS

All spies need to use coded messages to communicate vital information.
This alphabet code is the perfect way for beginner spies to get started!

To make your message unreadable, just switch each letter with the next letter in
the alphabet. For example, A becomes B, B becomes C, C becomes D, and so
on. (And if you want to write Z, just start at the beginning of the alphabet again,
so Z becomes A.)

So 'MEET ME AT SIX' becomes 'NFFU NF BU TJY'.

Can you work out what this means?

IFMQ! UIF CVSSPX JT TVSSPVOEFE!

TOP TIP
**To make your code harder, jumble
up the spaces between the words,
like this: NF FUNF B UTJY**

(TRANSLATION: MEET ME AT SIX)

MONTY'S MEERKAT BINGO

Why not try out Monty's Meerkat Bingo? It's a game for three players, and you can find out how to play below. Just cut out the boards and counters on the next page, and you're ready for some bingo fun!

1. Monty and his best friend, Micky, are going on a school trip to learn how to forage for food. Their teacher, Miss Melanie Meerkat, is in charge of the trip. Choose which of you will be Monty, which will be Micky, and which will be Miss Melanie Meerkat.

2. Monty and Micky should then choose either the backpack and counters with the school badge, or the ones with the school tie (see reverse of counters).

3. Without letting Miss Melanie Meerkat see, Monty and Micky choose three of their Things-to-Take counters and three of their Things-to-Find counters. They should place them all face-up on their backpack game boards.

4. Miss Melanie Meerkat then calls out in a random order three things that Monty and Micky need to take with them, and three things they need to find.

5. Each time Miss Melanie Meerkat says the name of an item that Monty or Micky has on their game boards, that player hands it to her. The winner is the first person to hand over all the items that are on their backpack game board to Miss Melanie Meerkat.

THINGS-TO-TAKE COUNTERS	THINGS-TO-FIND COUNTERS
• Poisonous plant book • Water bottle • Packed lunch • Paper and pens • Sunhat • Travel sweets	• Scorpion • Banana • Beetle • Egg • Snake • Lizard

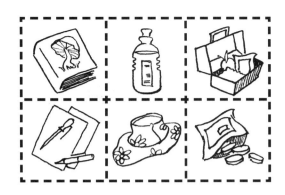

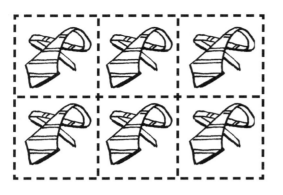

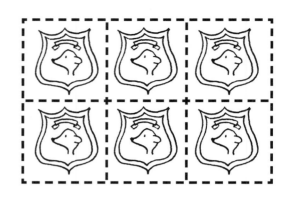

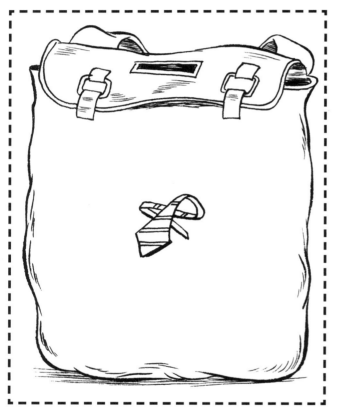

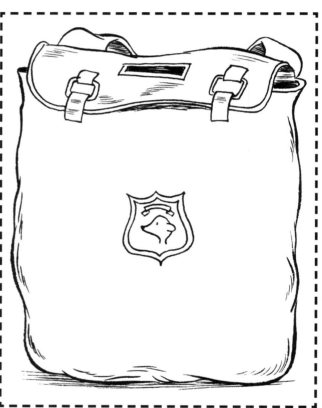

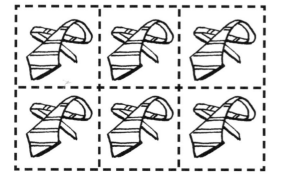

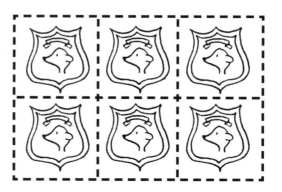

54

MAGIC MEERKAT MIND-READING

Read Monty's mind ...

... and draw what he is thinking about.

Monty has been amazing the meerkat triplets with his magic mind-reading. You can try this out yourself on a friend. All you need to do is give them the following five instructions.

1. Choose a number – any number.
2. Double it.
3. Add ten.
4. Divide it by two.
5. Subtract your original number from the new one.

Now place your hands on your friend's head and close your eyes as if you are reading his or her mind. Watch your friend's mouth drop open when you guess correctly the number in his or her head.

The secret of this trick is that the answer is always FIVE!

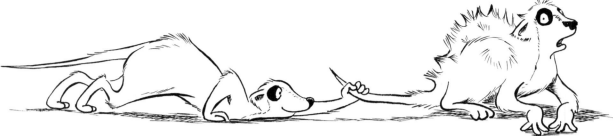

WHICH MEERKAT WOULD YOU BE?

Follow this fun flowchart to find out ...

You stick to Grub 'n' Chips. You know you like it, so why try anything else?

You go to the Oasis Café each week. What do you eat there?

You try a new dish each time you go – the weirder the better!

Rushing about, making lots of noise, playing sports and games all day.

START HERE

The whole family is having a picnic. What's the best thing about it?

Choosing a beautiful picnic spot, chatting and catching up with all the family news.

A surprise party, packed with lots of friends.

It's Magenta Meerkat's birthday. What do you give her?

Something personal and artistic that took you ages to make.

You're in charge of organizing everything and everyone.

The family is off for a day's canoeing. What's your role?

You came up with the idea to go canoeing but the details are up to someone else.

The lead, of course.

It's the meerkat school show next week. What part are you playing?

You're not into acting, but you're having fun as part of the backstage team.

Let her moan about how miserable she's feeling, then tell her some jokes.

Minnie Meerkat is stuck in bed with a sore paw. How do you cheer her up?

Bring books and music to take her mind off her paw, and make her a get-well card.

GRANDPA

You're the natural meerkat leader, dependable and organized. Your family know they can rely on you to make fun things happen. You have strong opinions and you're very wise. You're the one meerkats come to for advice.

MOLLY

You're the all-action meerkat. You're sporty, inquisitive and full of energy. You get yourself in a bit of trouble now and then, but you get away with things because you're so charming. Family life is never dull with you around!

MONTY

You're the most popular meerkat in the burrow! Everyone loves you because you're caring and kind and affectionate. You're fun to be around, and any meerkat who is feeling a bit blue will seek you out.

MELODY

You're the dreamy meerkat, creative and a deep thinker. You're happy on your own, but the family is important to you, too. You're the one who comes up with the loveliest, most thoughtful gifts on any special family occasion.

SANDY LANDING

Grandpa loves parachuting almost as much as juggling, but can you help him land his parachute safely? He's heading for some sinking sand, and there is only one square in the landing grid below that is safe to land on. Use the clue to help you. The answer is on page 64.

Decorate Grandpa's parachute.

Landing grid.

Clue: the square is white.
It is in a row with three purple squares and in a column with two black squares.

MEERKAT MOCKTAIL

This tasty mocktail is perfect for a thirsty meerkat. Read on to find out how to make one for yourself.

YOU WILL NEED:

- a tall glass
- half a lime
- ice
- a rolling pin
- a clean plastic food bag
- a handful each of raspberries and strawberries
- a sieve
- a fork
- 100 ml (½ cup) orange juice
- 100 ml (½ cup) sparkling water or lemonade
- a cherry, with the stalk left on.

1. Squeeze a little lime juice into the bottom of the glass.

2. Put ice cubes in a plastic bag, then bash the bag with a rolling pin to crush the ice. Add the ice to the glass.

3. Put the raspberries and strawberries in a sieve, above the glass. Crush the berries with a fork – that way the berries and juice go through, but the pips stay behind in the sieve.

4. Top up the glass with orange juice and fizzy water.

5. Pop a cherry on the top and serve with a straw.

TOP TIP

For an extra-special mocktail, add a scoop of vanilla ice cream on top and a sprig of mint to the edge of the glass.

HOME, SWEET HOME

Evenings are lots of fun in the meerkat burrow – but how many of these puzzles can you solve? Turn to page 64 to check your answers.

MEERKAT MOVIE NIGHT

The most popular meerkat movie of all is on TV tonight, starring a young meerkat wizard and his two friends. Which three of the images on the right are from the picture below?

A

B

C

D

E

F

HOW MANY MEERKATS?

How many meerkats (including images, statues and pictures of meerkats) can you spot in the burrow?

60

A. ....

B. ....

C. ....

D. ....

WHO'S WHO?

You've met all these meerkats before, but can you put the names in the frames?

E. ....

F. ....

G. ....
and ....

H. ....

ANSWERS

MEET MONTY
Pages 4 and 5

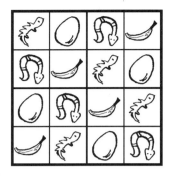

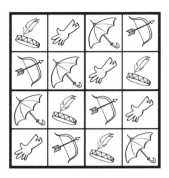

MEERKAT QUIZ
Page 6

1. c   3. a   5. b
2. b   4. b   6. a.

JUGGLING WITH GRANDPA
Page 9

The matching bow tie is C.

DOT-TO-DOT
Page 10

A lion is drinking at the water hole with the meerkats.

MOVIE MAYHEM
Pages 12 and 13

Balls A and C are the same.
Balls B and E are the same.
Balls D and G are the same.
Ball F is the ball that is unique.

Mimi had ice-cream sundae J, Molly had ice-cream sundae B.

A=1, B=2, C=4, D=3.

MELODY MEERKAT AND HER ORCHESTRA!
Pages 16 and 17

DESERT MUDDLE
Page 21

SPOT THE MEERKAT
Page 22

MONTY'S DREAM
Page 28

1. (**G**) Monty sees a long, strange shadow coming from behind a dune ...

2. (**A**) Monty creeps round the dune to see that the long, strange shadow is a small alien and his broken spaceship.

3. (**D**) Monty helps the alien mend the spaceship.

4. (**B**) They go whizzing up into space.

5. (**C**) They land on the alien's planet.

6. (**E**) They have a tea party on the alien's planet.

7. (**F**) Monty is dropped off back home and waves goodbye to the spaceship.

PARTY TIME!
Pages 30 and 31

Mimi and Molly are meerkats **B** and **D**.

A warthog is bursting out of Grandpa's cake.

RECORD HOLDERS
Page 35

Maurice Meerkat won Best Burrower.

Milly Meerkat won Star Sand Sculptor.

Magenta Meerkat won Top Trombonist.

Monty Meerkat won Superchef.

In height order from shortest to tallest: Maurice, Magenta, Milly, Monty.

JIGSAW JUMBLE
Page 38

The missing jigsaw pieces are **B**, **E** and **F**.

MEERKATS ON HOLIDAY
Pages 40 and 41

1. Meerkat **F** likes hang gliding, waterskiing and snorkelling, but not volleyball.

2. Meerkat **L** likes to play volleyball or go snorkelling but not waterskiing or hang gliding.

Meerkat **A** matches towel 2.
Meerkat **B** matches towel 1.
Meerkat **C** matches towel 4.
Meerkat **D** matches towel 3.

Meerkat **D** threw the beach ball that smashed Grandpa's Grub 'n' Chips.

Milly's meermaid is sand sculpture **B**.

GRANDPA'S ISLAND PUZZLER
Page 45

If Grandpa takes Milly across to the mainland, leaving Maurice and the coconut, he can return to the island, taking Maurice to the mainland. Then he can take Milly back to the island with him – and that way Maurice and Milly aren't left alone together. Next, Grandpa can leave Milly on the island and take the coconut across to the mainland, leaving it with Maurice. Finally, he can return to the island and take Milly back to the mainland.

WILDERNESS EXPLORERS!
Pages 46 and 47

1. SCORPION = C, 2. LIZARD = A,
3. MOUSE = D, 4. SNAKE = B.

1. D5	3. E1	5. A7
2. F1	4. B3	6. G4.

HIDE AND SEEK
Page 48

The triplets are hiding behind cactus E.

SPYKAT!
Pages 50 and 51

A. (9)   D. (7)   G. (2)

B. (5)   E. (3)

C. (4)   F. (5)

1. MAP IS UNDER FLOWERPOT
2. TRUST NO ONE
3. NAME OF TRAITOR IS SMITH
4. ATTACK DATE IS TUESDAY

Help! The burrow is surrounded!
The falcon has flown the nest.

SANDY LANDING
Page 58

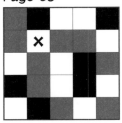

HOME SWEET HOME
Pages 60 and 61

Images **A**, **C** and **F** feature in the meerkat movie.

There are **17** meerkats hidden in this picture:

A. Monty	**D.** Margery	**G.** Molly
B. Melody	**E.** Mariella	and Mimi
C. The Triplets	**F.** Micky	**H.** Grandpa.

SNACK SPOTTER!

Monty's 16 grubs can be found on these pages ... did you spot them all?

• page 10 on top of a rock • page 16 on top of the horn-player's hairdo • page 19 above the cactus on the left of the page • page 23 bottom right of page between a small and a large rock • page 38 in the middle of the jigsaw, second piece from the right • page 39 next to the crabwalking meerkat • page 40 next to the starfish in the Match It! puzzle • page 41 as part of Grandpa's Grub 'n' Chips • page 41 next to sand sculpture E • page 46 between two sleeping meerkats • page 47 in box E3 • page 48 to the left of a cactus and next to some rocks • page 55 next to the rock • page 58 to the right of Grandpa's parachute • page 60 to the right of the sofa • page 61 in the frame on the top left.